Planning
That
Special
Day

Planning That Special Day

René Bédard

Library of Congress Control Number:		2010914564
ISBN:	Hardcover	978-1-4535-8832-1
	Softcover	978-1-4535-8831-4
	Ebook	978-1-4535-8833-8

This book was printed in the United States of America.

To order additional copies of this book, contact:
Xlibris Corporation
1-888-795-4274
www.Xlibris.com
Orders@Xlibris.com
86008

Contents

INTRODUCTION

Making sure nothing is forgotten or goes wrong for the wedding day you have been dreaming of, or wanting, is probably the most frightening. Every couple wants their wedding day to be remembered as being one of the best weddings ever attended! Careful planning is the key to achieving that goal.

To begin with, what is the meaning of a wedding? Regardless of your religion, a wedding is a couple's celebration of love for one another. It is a commitment made by the couple. This basic idea should not be forgotten during the planning stage. Keep in mind that anybody can have a party, and this is not just a party.

This book is a guide to help you make those wedding preparations. It is a helping hand along the way. Some suggestions might not apply to your situation or to the type of day you have planned, but they might help. Although the suggestions to be discussed will cover more than a one-year period, a wedding can be planned in less time with hard work and some luck!

Throughout this guide, you will be given a wide range of ideas and suggestions. Suggested time frames will be given, which should facilitate planning and probably avoid mistakes. These plans start from the moment you decide to get married to the final steps after the big day is over. You will also find some lists included for your convenience. These charts were included to help make things clearer and easier for you and also to give you a reference point.

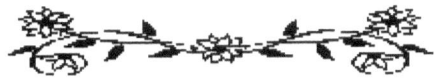

ENGAGEMENT

Congratulations and best wishes on your decision to get married. May the preparation on the road to your special day be fun and pleasant. Remember to stay calm and keep in mind the reason and purpose of your planning. Try to make the day as pleasant as possible for you and everyone else involved. Make an effort to avoid last-minute decisions. This will help keep the atmosphere and the mood calm.

Depending on your traditions and customs, you might want to have an engagement party. The engagement party is the perfect occasion to make your wedding decision public. You might decide to have a small gathering of the immediate family, or you might decide to have a big celebration by renting a gathering hall and inviting several guests. It all depends on what you want and what your budget will allow. The engagement party is also the perfect occasion for both sides of the families to get acquainted.

PREPARATIONS

Once the announcement of your wedding has been done, the planning really begins. It is recommended that you purchase a small package of accounting paper, along with 8.5 by 11 writing paper, and a calendar. An 8.5 × 11 envelope should also be purchased. The accounting paper will help you keep track of costs. It will also give you an up-to-date breakdown of the costs. The envelope is to ensure that all receipts are kept in one place. This will avoid searching everywhere for a receipt when you need it. You should assign a number to each receipt you get. These items should be put in some sort of organizer, such as a binder, in case other items need to be added as the planning progresses.

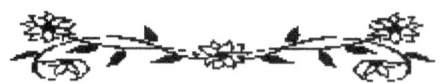

BUDGET

Before you start anything, you need to have a rough idea of the budget you will have. It is a good idea to know what you can spend before you start anything. You don't want to find out later that there are some things you cannot afford! By having a budget ahead of time, you will avoid future disappointment. It can be heartbreaking to find out at the last minute that you cannot afford something you really wanted.

It is a good idea to write a rough draft of the budget and to keep it in the organizer. It will be useful for future reference and will also help you remain within your spending limits. If a loan is needed, you will have time to plan for it.

INITIAL STEPS

Before you begin booking anything, an initial guest list should be drafted. The future bride and groom make a list of guests they would like to invite and so do the parents of the bride and groom. Keep in mind that this is an "initial" list. Once you have this list, you will need to decide on the size of the church and the hall. You want to make sure that you will have enough room for your guests. You also want to keep in mind the budget. For example, if your initial guest list is six hundred people, and you know that you will not be able to afford this, trim the guest list. You might need to trim your guest list more than once. Sometimes, some compromises need to be made between the bride, the groom, and their parents.

Once you have a guest list, you have to decide on a tentative wedding date. Why a tentative date? What if the hall or the church you want is not available on this date but is available a few days or a few weeks before or after your planned date? Do you change the planned date of your wedding? What if the hall or the church you want is too small or too big? What if it is too expensive? Do you rent another church or hall? The wedding date, the church, and the hall are the most important things; and they have to be coordinated and agreed upon. Once you have found a church and a hall on the decided date, you should give a deposit and get a receipt.

The receipt will be your confirmation of the booking. The receipt will have the date the booking was made and should have the date that you will be renting the premises. At a later date, if the premises are accidentally rented to someone else for the same day, your receipt will help put the odds in your favor.

For every receipt you will be getting when renting or booking something, get the date the receipt was made and the date of rental or booking. It only takes a few minutes more to get such a receipt, and it can avoid many problems.

All receipts should be assigned a number and put inside the envelope in the organizer. If you number your receipts, they will be easier to find. Once you get receipts for rentals or bookings, add the item on your accounting paper. This will help you keep a running table of expenses. Also, write down what has been done on your 8.5 × 11 writing paper.

When you give a deposit, it should be written, preferably on the receipt, when the balance of the amount is due. Add this to your calendar as soon as possible. By doing it this way, it is one less thing for you to remember. The calendar will remember for you! All you have to do is look at the calendar on a regular basis.

All this might sound complicated and tedious, but it is really simple. If all goes well, you can have a wedding date, a church, and a hall within thirty minutes. It might take a little longer if one of the premises has already been rented, or you decide to call around to compare prices. Once you have an agreement over the phone, schedule a meeting to give your deposit and get a receipt.

PROFESSIONAL SERVICES

Now would be a good time to look into a photographer and someone to record your event on video. Whether you decide to hire just one of these professionals or both, now is the perfect time to decide what to do. You can contact several of these professionals. Get some price quotes and compare some of the packages each one offers. Because it is still early, you can take your time. Look at their work. What is the quality of their work? You might even get a chance to watch them at work with a client. Try to contact some of their customers if you can. Find out what they liked and what they did not like. If some customers were not satisfied, maybe you can find out why. Also keep in mind the price of some of these professionals. You might not be able to afford what you want, but you might be able to work out some sort of arrangement with that person.

Something else to look into at this time is overall transportation. Do you want a limousine? You can look into various limousine services. You can compare prices and compare the services each one offers. If a limousine does not appeal to you, you can look into what you do find appealing. Would you rather have a horse-drawn carriage? Does someone you know have a special car or other means of transportation that interests you? What about decorations for your transportation? Some companies that offer these special services do not allow decorations or allow only a few of them. If you would like your transportation to be included in some pictures or in part of your video, this is something you can discuss with your service providers. Do not forget to keep your budget in mind when looking into the transportation part of your wedding day. You will probably be surprised when you find out how some of these specialty transportation services cost!

The next thing to do is to decide on the type of entertainment for your wedding day and during the evening. Is there a particular singer or group, such as relatives or friends, which you would like to perform during the wedding ceremony? Now would be a good time to ask them. If they agree, make it official by getting some sort of receipt even if it is a family member! What kind of entertainment do you want for the evening? Do you want a DJ or a band? Again, what about relatives or friends? When deciding on the entertainment, the amount they are charging could be a determining factor. It might be a good idea to look at your budget. Once they have agreed, again make it official by getting a receipt.

Give a deposit, if needed, for any of the above-mentioned services. Remember to get a receipt or something confirming the booking. This should be done even if you are booking friends or relatives. You would not want to end up without a photographer, video professional, transportation, or entertainment on your wedding day.

Once you get your receipt, follow the same recording process you did when the church and hall were rented.

Now is also a good time to decide on the catering. Will there be a meal at the hall? If yes, what will be on the menu? Will you have ham or roast with mashed potatoes, or will it be something else? Will the meal be a buffet style, or will it be served plates? Who will be preparing and serving this meal? These same decisions have to be made if you will have a light lunch during the evening. What will be served and by whom? You might want to make a few calls and compare prices. Don't forget to keep your budget in mind. If you will be hiring caterers, you might have one caterer for the meal and another caterer for the light lunch. Obtain receipts and go through the recording process.

In order to give you more flexibility and choice, it is recommended that the topics just discussed be done approximately twelve months prior to the wedding day. It might seem like a long time, but some gathering halls and professionals can be booked on certain dates for almost two or three years in advance. It is better to be safe than sorry! It can be disappointing when you call for a booking or rental, and they tell you: "Sorry, but we are already booked for that date!"

IMAGINE

Now that the main things are taken care of, here is a simple exercise that should help you with the remainder of your planning. You will need a pen, paper, and about thirty to sixty minutes of peace and quiet.

Make sure that you are by yourself or with your future spouse. Now, imagine every detail of your wedding, starting with the day before. Close your eyes and imagine your big day. Try to visualize every detail. As you visualize everything and everyone, make some notes.

Even if it seems like something minor or trivial, write it down to make sure you do not forget it. Picture yourself. Think of your wedding party. What about your parents? Think of the ceremony and the hall. Imagine how things will be placed. Add some decorations. This includes the color of the flowers, the flower arrangements, the decor, the food, etc. Try to go over everything step by step and write down as much as you can about what you are visualizing.

THE BRIDE

We have not discussed what is probably the most important person at your wedding day: the bride. Once the big decisions have been taken care of, such as the renting of the hall, it is time for the most important person of the day to go shopping. Keep in mind that everyone remembers the bride and her outfit. Enjoy this time. Look at various styles of wedding dresses. Look at catalogs and displays. Go to wedding shows. Do not be afraid to try various styles of wedding dresses and headpieces. Bring someone with you whose opinion you respect. As you try various dresses and headpieces, discuss them with this person. How did you feel in the dress or the headpiece? How did it look on you? Do not forget affordability. The bride's wardrobe should be decided and chosen six months to one year before the wedding day.

You might realize that you cannot buy what you really wanted! If that is the case, do not get disappointed. Keep looking. You just might find a similar style at a price that is within your budget.

You have now chosen your wedding dress and headpiece. Are alterations needed? If yes, plan some dates for your fittings. These dates should then be added to your calendar. The next step is to make financial arrangements with the supplier. Some suppliers might require full payment of the garments before beginning the alterations. Some might also include some alterations at no extra cost. If the supplier does the alterations for a fee, maybe you know someone who will be able to do them at a fraction of the cost! Whatever you do or decide, you have to make sure the garments will be available on your wedding day.

Remember to get a receipt and do your bookkeeping every time you give cash.

WEDDING PARTY

You need to decide who will be in your wedding party. Make sure the people you will ask to be in your wedding party are people you get along with. To begin with, decide on the size of your wedding party. Will you have a flower girl along with a ring bearer or just one of the two? What about junior bridesmaids? Who will be in your wedding party? This might sound very easy, but it could become difficult. Make sure you ask the people you want in your wedding party, and do not assume their answer.

Now that you have your wedding party and have an idea of what you would like, you need to decide on the style and color of the wedding party's attire. What kind of tuxedos will the men be wearing? Will the groom be wearing a tuxedo with a coattail or will it be a jacket? Will the groom's tuxedo be a different color than the ushers' tuxedos? What will the best man and ushers wear? Your best man has to be different than the ushers. Will the style of his tuxedo be like the groom's tuxedo but the same color as the ushers' tuxedos? Will his cummerbund be different? Will his corsage be different?

Because the tuxedos for the guys in the wedding party are often rented, whoever will be wearing a tuxedo should get measured for a proper fitting at least two months before the wedding.

What kind of dresses will the bridesmaids wear? Will the girls in the wedding party be wearing long, short, or cocktail length dresses? Like the best man, you probably want the maid of honor to be different somehow from the bridesmaids. It could be a different color of dress, different style of dress, different headpiece, or different flowers.

Unlike the men in the wedding party, the women do not have a few catalogs to look at and to choose from. Women usually have to go to various stores. Don't be afraid to try various styles and colors. Also study the material.

Keep in mind that what might look good on someone might not be right for someone else.

If everyone in the bridal party is to cover the cost of the outfits themselves, make sure everyone can afford what you are asking them to buy. Order the dresses and accessories for the maid of honor and bridesmaids early enough. Try to do this approximately six months or more before the wedding day. By taking care of this matter early, it gives you more time to shop around, which in turn, can solicit more ideas regarding these outfits. Also, if a special order has to be done or if several fitting sessions are required, it will give more time for everyone involved to take care of these matters. Don't forget to add the dates of the fitting sessions to your calendar. This way, you can remind your bridal party when there is a fitting session.

OTHERS

If there is someone else that should be outfitted for your wedding, don't forget to include them in this planning stage. This might include the parents of the bride and groom. It might even include a special guest such as a grandparent or a great-grandparent. You might need to take some time to go shopping with these people. It might just be a matter of reminding them that they need to be outfitted also. If fitting sessions are required, add the dates to your calendar. This way, you just need to remind them when the time comes. These people might also decide to take care of the fitting sessions themselves. This is something you will have to mutually agree upon.

DECORATING

By now, everybody should be outfitted for the occasion. It is time to start thinking about the decorations. You might want to concentrate on a certain theme or a particular color for your wedding day. For example, you might decide to go with swans or doves with a mixture of colors that would be the same as the bridesmaids' dresses. Also refer to the notes you wrote when you visualized your day. You might find that this makes it easier in deciding on how to decorate and what materials to use. Because decorating can involve so many things, let your imagination run wild. You might want to visit a few stores that specialize in decorations. They might have something unique, such as a display, which you can begin with and expand on. There are many things that you can use to decorate. These might include balloons, streamers, flowers, and table ornaments. You might also want to visit a few rental stores. Some rental stores carry such things as car decorations, wedding cakes (fake, of course), wishing wells, and arches. Renting some stuff might save you time and maybe some money! You might even want to carve the letters of the bride and groom's names on cardboard or Styrofoam. You might want to put these letters on a wall behind the wedding cake or in a corner especially decorated to take pictures. When deciding on your decorations, as with everything else, keep your budget in mind.

THE FORMAL INVITATION PACKAGE

Another big decision is the formal invitation package. Visit several stores and study various catalogs. This will give you the opportunity to study various styles and packages relating to the formal invitation. You might want to choose a package that coincides with your theme or color. You might also want the package's color to match the color of the bridesmaids' dresses. You will be amazed at the variety of packages that are available. The most difficult part will be deciding on which package you will take. A typical package might include the following:

1. Formal invitations
2. Reply cards
3. Return envelopes
4. Reception cards
5. Thank you cards
6. Napkins
7. Matches

Some packages might include some supplies to put a wedding keepsake together. The keepsake might include some candy, some cake, or anything else you might have in mind, along with the name of the new couple and the date of their wedding day attached to it. If you have something else in mind for the keepsake, now is the time to decide what you will have.

Once the package has been decided upon, along with the design and lettering style, the actual wording of the formal invitation and other related items has to be chosen. If you have guests that speak different languages, will the wording be bilingual? Will you have a different set of the package for each language, or will the package be bilingual? Which address will be on the return envelopes?

Make sure to order a few more items than you actually need from each category of the package. You might want a complete set for yourself and the parents. It makes a great souvenir! The extra items also enable you to correct mistakes you might make when preparing your individual sets for mailing. Some people who are great craft makers might ask you for a set because of something they are working on. It is also a good idea to have too many of the formal invitation packages, than not enough!

WEDDING EXTRAS

Your guests should receive their individual formal invitation two to three months before the wedding. Your reply card should include a "deadline" date for your guests to reply. Your guests should have about four weeks from the date of mailing to decide if they will be attending your wedding or not and mail in their reply. The date of the mailing and the reply date should be included in your calendar.

Depending on your budget, you might want other things, such as the following:

1. Guest book
2. Wedding pen
3. Wedding knife
4. Bride server (for the cake)
5. Champagne glasses

Will you get a fancy wedding pen for your guests to sign the guest book, or will they use a regular pen? Will you take champagne glasses for the bride and groom only, or will everyone in the wedding party get such a glass?

The formal invitation package and the extras mentioned above can probably be ordered from the same place. If that is the case, verify everything when it arrives very carefully. Check every word and date. You do not want spelling mistakes or the wrong date to be printed. Is everything the same style and color you ordered? If there is anything wrong, bring it to the attention of your supplier as soon as possible so arrangements can be made to correct the problem. If you will not be purchasing the extras at the same place as the formal invitation package, you will have to shop around a little more. You will also have to remember what items were ordered from which place. This is something that should be in your notes on the 8.5 × 11 writing paper.

You might want to start looking into the formal invitation package and extras approximately six months before the wedding day. Again, this gives you plenty of time to shop around and to correct any problems you might encounter.

THE INVITATION

It is now time to send out your formal invitation. As mentioned earlier, you might want to put a few complete sets aside as souvenirs for yourselves, your parents, and the guests who requested one. You might also want to send a formal invitation to your bridal party. Also make sure you have the correct spelling of every guest's name. Do you plan on personally delivering each invitation to your guests? Probably not. Therefore, you will have to make sure you have the correct mailing address of each guest. You will probably be sending the formal invitation, a reply card, and a return envelope professionally printed. If you want the address of each guest professionally printed on the package, you will have to make arrangements with your supplier. You might also decide to "personalize" each individual package by writing your guests' addresses yourself. It is also a good idea to put a stamp on the return envelope. In other words, your guests should just have to answer on the reply card, insert it in the reply envelope, seal the envelope, and drop it in a mailbox. Remember, the formal invitation should be sent approximately two to three months before your wedding day. Keep in mind that your reply card has a final reply date. Therefore, the mailing date, which was decided upon ordering and which you also added to your calendar, should be adhered to.

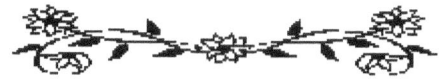

ATTENDANCE

Keep a list of guests who were sent a formal invitation. You might also keep a running total of guests who will attend. Including a number, meaning number of guests who will attend, under each guest's name and address easily addresses this issue.

ADDRESSES OF GUESTS

NAME: _____

ADDRESS: _____

CITY: _____

POSTAL/ZIP CODE: _____

NUMBER OF ATTENDEES: _____

At the bottom of each page, you could have a total for the number of guests attending for that page. When you receive a reply, you update your NUMBER ATTENDING for that particular guest or family. Afterward, update your TOTAL at the bottom of the page. If you have several pages of guests, you just add your TOTALs at the bottom of each page to know exactly how many are attending. You could also have only one TOTAL at the very end of your guest list that would be updated upon receipt of a reply. This will give you an up-to-date number of guests that will be attending by looking at just one number. You could also keep numbers of guests attending on behalf of the groom and guests attending on behalf of the bride.

SECONDARY GUESTS

Once you have reached your reply "deadline," check your guest list for outstanding replies. You might want to contact those guests by phone, or via a personal visit, to get their reply. Once you have everyone's answer, find out how many extra seats you will have at your reception. You get this amount by finding out the total number of seats available and total number of guests attending. You might then return to your original guest list and contact some of the guests you had originally omitted from your "final" guest list. Why have empty seats? You are paying for those seats, why not fill them up. Due to time constraints, you might want to contact some of these "secondary" guests by phone or personal visit. To avoid confrontation and also avoid upsetting friends and relatives, you could tell them that you made a mistake and forgot to include them in your guest list. You could also tell them the truth and explain to them that you have extra seats and would like them to attend. Only you know how they will react.

Once some of these "secondary" guests have been contacted and have agreed to attend, include their name and address on your guest list. Then add them to your running total of guests attending.

Your total number of guests attending will be useful when contacting your caterer or caterers. The mailing address of your guests will be useful when sending your "Thank you" cards. You will not have to look up any of the mailing addresses because you will already have this information.

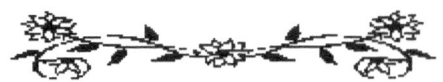

MASTER OF CEREMONY

You must decide if you will have a master of ceremony. The master of ceremony is the spokesperson for basically everything and everyone. That person is the intermediary between you and your guests and vice versa. Quite often, the master of ceremony is the person who will entertain the guests when the bride and the groom cannot do so. For example, if there is a time you are away for pictures, it is up to that person to entertain the guests. Also, while you are enjoying the meal, the master of ceremony will often entertain your guests. This person will often entertain the guests by telling stories, either humorous and/or sentimental, about the bride and groom. For these reasons, try to choose someone who is comfortable with public speaking, interesting to listen to, and also knows the bride and groom quite well. It is enjoyable listening to someone who is enthusiastic, funny, and also sentimental when the moment asks for it. The master of ceremony usually has a schedule of the day's events, a sitting plan, and a list of special guests you would like to acknowledge.

THE MEAL

You also have to decide on the type of meal you will have. Will it be a buffet style or served plates? No matter what type of meal you have, the head table should always be served first. If the bride and/or groom would like, or needs, a special meal (probably because of dietary reasons), advise your caterer. Wine is usually served with the meal. You might want to buy special wine glasses for the bride and groom and the guests at the head table. This depends on your budget. Depending on your religion and tradition, the guests will do various things to make the bride and groom kiss or put them in the spotlight. Have fun and go with it. It is YOUR day after all!

Once the head table has almost finished the meal, it is at this point, quite often, the master of ceremony plays its most important role. This is usually where the "entertaining" occurs. Besides his little anecdotes, the master of ceremony must not forget to introduce the head table, then the special guests you want to acknowledge. It would also be considered common courtesy to thank your caterer, photographer, and anyone else whom you either hired or asked for help. The master of ceremony should also not forget to "toast" the new couple. He might even ask some guests to say a few words. Finally, the new bride and groom should also say a few personal words. Do not be afraid to thank your guests for attending your wedding. Once the meal is done and the speeches have been said, the master of ceremony should inform the guests as to what is next on the agenda.

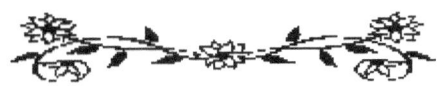

THE NIGHT BEFORE

What usually happens next is the formal reception and the dance. If possible, try to do some of the preparations before the big day itself. For example, if this part of the wedding will be held in a hall, try to decorate the hall the night before. If this part of the wedding will be done outside, make sure everything is ready.

If the reception and the dance will be held indoors, try to make arrangements to decorate the night before. This gives you plenty of time to decorate the way you want in a relaxing atmosphere. You will not be under pressure to decorate within a limited time frame. The last thing on your mind during your wedding day should be the decorations at the hall for your reception and dance. If possible, try to arrange the tables for the meal also. Place the head table with the right amount of chairs and arrange the table ornaments. Don't forget to prepare a table for the wedding cake. What about a table for your gifts? If you have a "wishing well" for your cards, you might want to set this up close to the table you have set up for the gifts. If you will have people greeting your guests as they arrive, make sure their area is also ready. If you have a guest book, where will you put it? If you will have some finger foods or other types of snacks for your guests during the evening, where will these snacks be located? Here are a few tables you might consider setting up:

1. Head table
2. Cake table
3. Gifts table
4. Tickets table
5. Guest book table
6. Wishing well table
7. Table for snacks during evening

One event to consider, which often occurs during the formal reception, is the cutting of the wedding cake. It is a great time to take pictures. For this reason, you might want some special decorations for this table. Keep your background in mind while decorating. Depending on what will be in the background where the cake cutting will take place, you might want to make or rent a special background.

Another thing to consider is whether or not you will have a "receiving line." If you will have a receiving line, when will it take place? Will you have it before the formal reception or before the evening starts? Where will the receiving line be? Will you have it at the entrance so you can greet your guests as they come in? Will the receiving line be greeting the guests before or after they have signed the guest book? Who will be in the receiving line? Of course, the new bride and groom will be included. What about their parents? What about the wedding party?

Do not leave money, tickets, or other important extras (such as wedding glasses) out in the open. Try to lock them someplace where they will quickly be accessible when you need them. It can be disappointing to arrive at your reception on your wedding day and find that some things are missing.

If you will be selling tickets for beverages, decide on the price, write it down, and store it with the rest of your stuff. If beverages will be bought directly from the bar and prices have been predetermined by the establishment, you have nothing to do. However, if your input will be required to determine the prices, the meeting to settle this should have been done prior to this night. What you should now do is write the prices agreed upon and store this with the rest of your stuff. This is to be given to the bartenders the day of the wedding.

If anything else will be sold, either at the reception or at the dance, now would be a good time to determine prices. Include a price list and a cash box. Once this has been done, include these items with your stuff to be used on the wedding day. It will be a busy evening. Better to do it now, than having to do it on your wedding day.

You might want to put the "best man" or "maid of honor," or both, in charge of the things you will store away until the next day. By putting them in charge, these are a few less things for you to worry about.

THE REHEARSAL

Another thing that will probably be done the night before your wedding day is the wedding rehearsal. You will need to decide who will attend the rehearsal. You want to keep your attendees to a minimum. After all, it is just a rehearsal! The people who should attend are the following:

1. Bride and groom
2. Wedding party
3. Parents of the bride and groom
4. Person who will perform the ceremony
5. Person(s) who will do the readings
6. Musicians
7. Others who are part of the ceremony

You might also decide to have your photographer present. What about the person you hired to record your wedding? Keep in mind that if you want the professionals you hired to attend, they might charge you an extra fee. You will probably have to consider your budget when making this decision.

DRAWS AND TRADITIONS

Sometimes, some prizes are also "offered" during the dance portion of the evening. You might want your guests to sign a special paper when entering. Then you can draw a name, or names, and give away some prizes as a gesture of thanks. You might also want to sell raffle tickets for the prize or prizes. If you decide to have some prize drawn with raffle tickets, you will need to decide on the type of prizes that will be drawn. Then, make sure you have those prizes. You will need to make sure you have plenty of tickets available. Then, decide on the ticket prices. Remember to have a container of some sort to put the tickets inside for the draw. The ticket prices should also be included in the stuff you will store away at the hall. This was discussed earlier. You then have to decide at which time during the evening these prizes will be drawn. If you will have more than one draw, decide on a time for each one.

Other things to consider are more "traditional" ceremonies. These ceremonies also have to be planned into the evening. This would include the bride's throwing of the bouquet. What about the groom's removing and throwing of the bride's garter? Some might include a garter for the groom, which the bride removes and throws. You might also include some religious ceremonies. If some sort of religious ceremonies should take place, make sure to plan for them. Remember that you want everything to be perfect.

THE LATE LUNCH

In some areas, it is required by law that your guests are offered something to eat before leaving a social event such as this one. This is often done approximately one hour before the bar is closed. You should find out what the law stipulates for your area. You might want to have a light meal as a gesture of thanks for your guests. If a meal will be served at the end of the evening, you will have to decide if it will be a cold and/or hot meal. You will then have to make proper arrangements to make sure the meal is ready. Will you be hiring a caterer? This will depend on your budget. If you decide to hire the services of a caterer, will the caterer take care of everything? Will there be something that you will have to take care of? If you will not be hiring a caterer and will be preparing this meal yourself (with some help, of course), you have to plan the preparation of this meal. You will also have to make sure the meal is properly stored away. Make sure you have all the necessary supplies for this meal. These supplies might include the following:

1. Plates and cups
2. Napkins
3. Utensils
4. Table clothes
5. Beverages (coffee, tea, juice, and etc.)
6. Beverage accessories (milk, sugar, stir sticks, and etc.)
7. Salt and pepper
8. Condiments
9. Ice

The kitchen staff of the hall you are renting might decide to help you for an extra fee. It will be up to you to decide.

HONEYMOON

Another important decision that has to be planned is the honeymoon. First, you have to decide where you will be going. You might decide that you will not be taking a trip after all. If you are planning to take a trip for your honeymoon, make sure the proper reservations and bookings have been done. Make sure that everything you will need is packed and ready to go. When you are ready to leave for your honeymoon, you should just have to pick up your luggage. This leads to the next decision that has to be made: When will you be leaving for your honeymoon? Will you be leaving at the end of the evening? Will you be leaving the next day? Will you be leaving a few days later? If you will be leaving at the end of the evening, where will you go to change from your wedding clothes to your traveling clothes? Once you have changed, will you return to the hall? If you will be leaving at the end of the evening, you will have to make sure someone will be in charge of a few things while you are gone. Where will the gifts and cards you received be stored during your absence? Who will return the supplies you have rented? Who will be in charge of your cash receipts? If you were responsible for supplying beverages for the bar, who will remove those beverages from the premises? These are important decisions, and you will have to delegate these duties to people you trust.

If you will be leaving for your honeymoon the day after, where will you be spending your wedding night? You might want to inform someone of your plans. This way, you can still be reached in case of an emergency.

THE DAY AFTER

Something else to consider is the day after the wedding day. After your big day, there is still a bit of planning that is needed. Everybody does things differently. One suggestion is to have a gathering at either the bride's or the groom's parents place. This gives family and friends a chance to get together and celebrate, one more time, the event they witnessed the day before. If you have not left for your honeymoon, this is a good opportunity to personally thank your guests.

Something else you might consider doing on this day is opening the gifts and cards you received the night before. If you will be doing this, it is quite easy to forget what each person or couple gave you. After all, there is a lot going on! One thing you might want to do is write down who gave you what present on a piece of paper. For the cards, you can easily write their names on the inside of the cards. If there is a card attached to a gift, write what the gift was inside the card and attach the card with the gift. Get someone to help you. As you are opening the gifts or the cards, this person can write everything down and even keep a running total of the cash you receive. Try and put the gifts on display afterward if it is possible. This will help satisfy your guests' curiosity, and it is also a sign of appreciation! Once this is done, you basically have the rest of the day to relax and enjoy yourself.

CONCLUSION

Throughout this guide, you were given a wide range of ideas and suggestions. Suggested time frames were given to help facilitate planning and avoid mistakes. This book guided you in making those wedding preparations. Remember, if you feel that a suggestion does not apply to your situation or the type of day you have planned, do what you feel best applies toward your vision of your wedding day. While the wedding preparations were taking place, hopefully the basic idea of a wedding was not forgotten. Remember that a wedding is a couple's celebration of love for one another. With the careful planning you have put into this day, may your wedding day be everything you have ever dreamed of and more!

AS SOON AS POSSIBLE

❖ Book the church and the hall. Make sure both are available at the same date.
❖ Choose the type of wedding and the atmosphere of your wedding.
❖ Decide on the number of guests that you would like to attend.
❖ Make a budget.
❖ Book the photographer.
❖ Decide on the entertainment for the evening. Will it be a DJ or a band?
❖ Book a video recording professional.
❖ Select transportation.
❖ Decide on the size of the wedding party.
❖ Select the people you would like to be in your wedding party.
❖ Select caterer.
❖ Shop for wedding dress and headpiece.

SIX MONTHS

❖ Make final guest list including guests from both the bride's and groom's side of the family.
❖ Decide on dresses for bridesmaids.
❖ Purchase dresses for bridesmaids.
❖ Inquire about bar.
  ➢ Your responsibility or hall's responsibility
  ➢ Inquire about bartenders
  ➢ Open or closed bar
  ➢ Price of alcoholic beverages
  ➢ Tickets for alcoholic beverages
    o Bride and groom's stamp on them?
❖ Select church singers and music.
❖ Publication of wedding.
  ➢ Church paper, newspaper, or etc.
❖ Select the wedding invitation package.
❖ Select the type of keepsake. Order them or buy supplies to make them.

TWO TO THREE MONTHS

- ❖ Send out invitations.
- ❖ Decide on master of ceremony.
- ❖ Book babysitter(s), if needed.

ONE MONTH

- ❖ Select hairdresser.
  - ➢ Book appointment
  - ➢ Decide on the style of hair to go with the headpiece
  - ➢ Try several different hairstyles with headpiece
- ❖ Choose readings and vows.
- ❖ Select prizes for the draws and the price of the tickets.
- ❖ Choose person(s) in charge of money, gifts, and cards for the evening.
- ❖ Decide on the decorations for the hall, church, etc.
- ❖ Obtain marriage license, if needed.

WEEK BEFORE

- ❖ Pick up wedding dress.
- ❖ Pick up attire of the wedding party.
- ❖ Prepare a "thank you" package for the wedding party and give it to them on rehearsal night.
- ❖ Package might include the following:
  - ➢ Invitation, matches, napkins
  - ➢ Keepsake
  - ➢ Present
- ❖ Decide when to give keepsakes on wedding day.
- ❖ Call photographer and/or video professional to confirm time.
- ❖ Confirm musician(s), florist, cake, motel rooms, etc.

- ❖ Make sure bride has everything she needs.
  - ➢ Lingerie, panty hose, shoes, etc.
- ❖ Make itinerary for wedding day.

DAY AND NIGHT BEFORE

- ❖ Make sure cars are clean.
- ❖ Try to decorate cars.
- ❖ Pick up rented decorations; designate someone to pick them up.
- ❖ Go over speeches.
- ❖ Confirm rehearsal time with wedding party and others attending.
- ❖ Invite the wedding party and others involved in the ceremony for a gathering after the rehearsal.
- ❖ Explain the events of the wedding day at the "rehearsal party."
- ❖ Great occasion to give "thank you" gift to the wedding party.
- ❖ Try to decorate and arrange hall.
- ❖ Prepare wedding dress, headpiece, and accessories needed.
- ❖ Have a good night's sleep.

WEDDING DAY

- ❖ Make sure the bride goes to hair appointment.
- ❖ Make sure rings are at church or with the best man.
- ❖ Keepsakes placed at plates or ready to hand out.
- ❖ Pay priest or clergyman (best man, father of the bride or groom).
- ❖ Pay ceremony musicians.
- ❖ Get dressed.
- ❖ Enjoy and relax.

DANCE AND MEAL

- ❖ Have itinerary done for the master of ceremony.
- ❖ Prepare sitting plan for head table.

- ❖ Pay those requiring payment such as bartenders, caterers, etc.
- ❖ Prepare table for gifts and wedding cake.
- ❖ Make sure all is ready for late lunch.

DAY AFTER

- ❖ Reception and opening of the gifts.
- ❖ Record presents and monies received.
- ❖ Put gifts on display.
- ❖ Personally thank as many guests as you can.
- ❖ OPTIONAL: serve a meal or buffet.

STATIONARIES

1. Wedding guest book
2. Garter
3. Tickets for alcoholic beverages
4. Tickets for door prize(s) and draw prize(s)
5. Ring bearer pillow
6. Decorations for hall
   - ➢ Streamers, balloons, scotch tape, etc.
7. Wedding cake
8. Liquor license
9. Invitations
   - ➢ How many
   - ➢ Wording
   - ➢ Reply cards
   - ➢ Return envelopes
   - ➢ Reception cards
   - ➢ Thank you cards
10. Napkins
11. Keepsakes
12. Matches
13. Wedding knife and cake server
14. Pen
15. Stamps

16. Champagne glasses
    - ➢ Bride and groom
    - ➢ Wedding party
    - ➢ Parents of bride and groom
17. Basket, or wishing well, for wedding cards
18. Car decorations
19. Cash box with some change

—*NOTES*—

—NOTES—

—*NOTES*—

—NOTES—

—*NOTES*—

—NOTES—